HISTORY'S GREATEST WARRIORS

SAMURAI

WARLORDS OF JAPAN

Cavendish Square
New York

Published in 2015 by Cavendish Square Publishing, LLC
243 5th Avenue, Suite 136, New York, NY 10016

First Edition

Library of Congress Cataloging-in-Publication Data

Dawson, Patricia (Patricia Adelaide)
Samurai : warlords of Japan / Patricia Dawson.
pages cm. — (History's greatest warriors)
Includes index.
ISBN 978-1-50260-125-4 (hardcover) ISBN 978-1-50260-123-0 (ebook)
1. Samurai—Japan—Juvenile literature. I. Title.

DS827.S3D39 2015
952'.02—dc23

2014028064

Editor: Amy Hayes
Copy Editor: Cynthia Roby
Art Director: Jeffrey Talbot
Designer: Joseph Macri
Senior Production Manager: Jennifer Ryder-Talbot
Production Editor: David McNamara
Photo Researcher: J8 Media

The photographs in this book are used by permission and through the courtesy of:
Cover photo by KAZUHIRO NOGI/AFP/Getty Images; Usiwakamaru/File:AntokuTennou Engi.7&8 Dannoura Kassen.jpg/Wikimedia Commons, 4; Steven Wynn/iStock/Thinkstock, 7; Print Collector/Hulton Archive/Getty Images, 8; DEA/A. DAGLI ORTI/De Agostini/Getty Images, 12; Unknown/File:Minamoto no Yoshitsune.jpg/Wikimedia Commons, 13; Mary Evans/BeBa/Iberfoto, 14; Unknown/File:Kumagai Naozane and Taira no Atsumori.jpg/Wikimedia Commons, 18; Felice Beato/The Bridgeman Art Library/Getty Images, 21; Ogata Gekko/File:Ōishi Sezaemon Nobukiyo.jpg/Wikimedia Commons, 23; Laurascudder/File:Portland Japanese gardens zen garden.jpg/Wikimedia Commons, 25;Private Collection/© Look and Learn/Bridgeman Images/Getty Images, 26; Unknown/Library of Congress/File:Samurai on horseback.png/Wikimedia Commons, 29; Toyokuni III/Kunisada/File:Rooftop battle.jpg/Wikimedia Commons, 30; Unknown/The Japanese book "Kennin-ji: The Oldest Zen Temple in Kyoto"/File:Akamatsu Masanori.jpg/Wikimedia Commons, 33; Unknown/PawełMM/File:Chushingura Matsu no Oroka.JPG/Wikimedia Commons, 34; Felice Beato/Hulton Archive/Getty Images, 36; Print Collector/Hulton Archive/ Getty Images, 39; Print Collector/Hulton Archive/Getty Images, 40; Hulton Archive/Getty Images, 41; TOHO/Album/Newscom, 43.

Printed in the United States of America

CONTENTS

The battle of Dannoura was fiercely fought by some of the most highly-trained warriors in history.

Samurai warriors began more or less as bodyguards who protected wealthy landowners. However, they became much more than that, and their presence transformed Japanese society. The first full-time warriors, the samurai and their fighting skills brought peace and order to Japan. Samurai became a beacon of justice in society, living by a strict code of honor. However, it could not last.

The samurai did their job well, and soon powerful groups of samurai began to form. Eventually, there were two groups far more powerful than the rest—the Taira and the Minamoto. It was bound to happen. Eventually the two sides would have to clash. Both the Taira and the Minamoto believed they who should rule all of Japan. Soon, a bloody war began.

The two sides battled, with archers raining down arrows on their enemies. Skilled fighters engaged in hand-to-hand combat, as each side would brandish their signature swords, looking for battles to bring honor to their **clans** and ancestors. At first, the Taira clan had the advantage, but the Minamoto would not give up. For five years, the two sides battled. Minamoto Yoshitune was finally able to defeat the rival Taira clan at the battle of Dan-No-Ura. After numerous battles between the warriors on both sides, it was a naval battle that ended this five-year conflict. Yoshitune was the new leader of Japan. Custom dictated that the warriors on the losing side take their own life through **seppuku**.

The samurai were the legendary **medieval** warrior class of Japan. For more than one thousand years, they were the soldiers, peacekeepers, and rulers of Japan. The samurai lived exciting, violent, and often short lives. In times of war, they were fierce fighters, battling to the death in the service of their masters. In peacetime, they were gentlemen who appreciated poetry, philosophy, and finely crafted works of art. During many times in their history, samurai were landlords. Many men worked in their service, guarding or farming the samurai's prized lands.

While samurai are usually remembered for their sword fighting skills, they were also great archers.

Samurai warriors wore lots of armor to protect them in battle. Only people from rich families could become samurai, in part because of the expensive armor they wore.

CHAPTER ONE

THE SAMURAI WARRIORS OF JAPAN

Samurai, in the Japanese language, means "those who serve." The term was first used to describe professional warriors sometime between the ninth and eleventh centuries. Unlike the warriors before them, who would serve as farmers during peaceful eras, the samurai was a new breed of warrior. They were full-time soldiers who only trained to fight. These powerful fighters would be an important part of Japan's history for the next eight centuries.

Samurai were usually from well-to-do families. Since they did not have to work to support themselves, they had more time to train as soldiers. Samurai were chosen to serve based on their skills at riding horses and using weapons. Young men chosen to be samurai were expected to perform their duty and train in the arts of war. They were also expected to be ready for battle at any time.

BUSHIDO TIP

Women had an important role as members of the samurai class. Wives of samurai needed to be well trained in **martial arts** because they often defended their homes from attacks.

In some cases, women fought alongside the male samurai in battle. One of the most well-known of these fierce female warriors was Tomoe Gozen. She earned her fame in battle in the late twelfth century.

Most early samurai banded together in clans. A clan is a large group of families. The samurai gave his loyalty to the clan leader. In return for loyal service, the leader loaned portions of his land to his samurai.

Land was important to the samurai because all wealth in Japan was based upon the production of rice. The clan leader received his land from a provincial governor. Each provincial governor was appointed to rule over a specific region of Japan. The provincial governor received his land from the imperial government, or government ruled by the emperor. The emperor ruled all of Japan.

The Two Great Samurai Clans

By the beginning of the twelfth century, two samurai clans had risen to positions of great power. These two groups were the Minamoto and the Taira. The Minamoto and the Taira, like many clans, served the imperial government. They helped Japan's emperor to defeat any clans who threatened his government. In return for their service, the emperor rewarded the Minamoto and Taira clans with large amounts of land. The wealth provided by this land allowed the Minamoto and Taira to become very powerful. In time, they became almost as powerful as the imperial government for which they fought.

This screen depicts the Gempei War, a war fought between the two most powerful clans of samurai.

In the mid-twelfth century, the Taira clan plotted to take control of the imperial government. Taira Kiyomori was the leader of the Taira clan. People of the Taira clan married into families of the imperial government. They took powerful positions within the government. By 1160, they had all but destroyed the Minamoto clan and had full control of Japan. By 1180, Kiyomori had placed his grandson on the emperor's throne. However, the Minamoto soon rallied their forces, beginning the Gempei War.

Minamoto no Yoshitsune is one of the most famous samurai. He was an important leader during the clash between the Taira and the Minamoto.

Five Years of Fighting

The battles fought between the Minamoto and the Taira are known as the Gempei War.

Much of the Gempei War was fought around the Uji River and the sea. Fighting in the water became an important battle strategy for the samurai.

The war began outside of Kyoto, a city in the west, on the mainland of Japan. At first, the war went badly for the Minamoto. Their earliest attack was poorly planned. The Minamoto were forced to retreat from a huge Taira army across the Uji River, south of Kyoto. Once across the river, they destroyed a section of the Uji Bridge so that the Taira could not cross on horseback.

While the two armies shot arrows at each other from the riverbanks, samurai fought in hand-to-hand combat on the bridge. Many samurai fought to the death on the Uji Bridge.

The Taira force gathered its strength and crossed the river. They soon overpowered the Minamoto. Many Minamoto were killed while others fled to safety.

As the Gempei War continued, the Minamoto slowly gained the upper hand. Under the leadership of Minamoto Yoshitsune, the Minamoto were able to wear down the Taira army. The Minamoto drove the Taira off the mainland of Japan.

The final battle of the war was fought at sea, in the Straits of Shimonoseki. During this battle, the Minamoto destroyed the Taira fleet and completely wiped out the Taira army. By defeating the Taira, the Minamoto became the strongest clan in Japan. This allowed the Minamoto to break away from the imperial government and form its own government. Its leader was more powerful than the emperor. He was a samurai warrior known as the **shogun**.

The Shogun's Control of Japan

By the late twelfth century, the shoguns took control of Japan. They ruled for nearly six hundred years. During the reign of the shogun, Japan still had an emperor. However, he was more of a symbol of Japanese tradition. The shogun held the real power.

After taking control, the shogun owned all of the land. They loaned parts of it to powerful samurai known as **shugo**. The shugo, in turn, loaned land to less powerful samurai who served under them. As long as the shogun was strong enough to control the shugo, he could control all the samurai of Japan.

Between the twelfth and seventeenth centuries, samurai from different clans struggled to gain power over one another. If a samurai was strong enough to bring all clans under his control, he could claim the prized title of shogun. A shogun had to work hard to keep control over the shugo and their samurai.

The shogun was under constant pressure to keep the shugo under his control. To prevent shugo from plotting against him, a shogun would take members of the shugo's family as **hostages**. To keep their families safe, most shugo would not dare rebel. The shogun would also require the shugo to live in the shogun's capital city during part of every other year. The shogun could then keep an eye on his subordinate samurai.

To kill his enemies from a distance, a samurai would sharpen his archery skills and marksmanship.

CHAPTER TWO

THE WEAPONS OF THE SAMURAI

A samurai was trained to use a variety of weapons. When a samurai fought, he chose his weapon according to the type of battle. Most battles began far away from the opponent. For fighting from a distance, the samurai mastered the bow and arrow. Eventually, the invention of gunpowder made its way to Japan. The samurai adapted, adding the powerful **harquebus** rifle to his arsenal of weapons.

When samurai needed to fight an opponent at close range, hand-to-hand combat would begin. Samurai used weapons such as spears, called *yari*, and the *naginata*, a long, curved blade attached to the end of a pole. The most famous of samurai weapons is the sword. The most recognized samurai sword is called the *katana*. A single-edged sword, the katana has become the most lasting symbol of the samurai.

Dressed for Battle

Throughout their long history, samurai always wore some form of armor. Early samurai wore armor called *yoroi*. This protective gear had to be strong and lightweight. It needed to be light so that the horse upon which the samurai rode would not have too much weight to carry.

Yoroi armor was made of small plates of iron bound together with cords of silk or leather. The plates were sewn into horizontal strips. These strips were then sewn together to make the entire suit of armor. When finished, the armor had a boxlike appearance. It was often painted black, and the cords were usually brightly colored.

This man is pictured wearing traditional Yoroi armor. He uses a katana sword, the famously deadly sword of the samurai.

Other pieces of armor completed the suit. Heavy shoulder plates, called *sode*, were worn on the upper arms. The rest of the arms were covered by long, cloth sleeves. These sleeves were covered with iron plates that were sewn in place. Sometimes, the right arm was left uncovered. This helped the samurai to easily use his bow. The helmet was a heavy metal bowl made of plates of iron joined together. Most helmets had a neck guard attached. Later styles of armor featured a more flexible design, which was necessary for samurai when they fought on foot with swords.

BUSHIDO TIP

According to Japanese legend, the great samurai warrior Minamoto Yoshitsune learned his sword-fighting skills from forest goblins, called *tengu*. These goblins were described as half-man and half-bird.

The Bushido Code

The samurai lived following a strict code of conduct. This code, which became known as **Bushido**, stressed the ideals of honor and duty. A samurai was expected to defend the honor of his clan. When necessary, he was also expected to give his life for the wellbeing of his master. The samurai's master was usually a shogun or shugo. Failure to serve one's master with complete loyalty was considered a disgrace. To most samurai, disgrace was considered a worse fate than death. In many cases, a samurai would take his own life rather than live in disgrace.

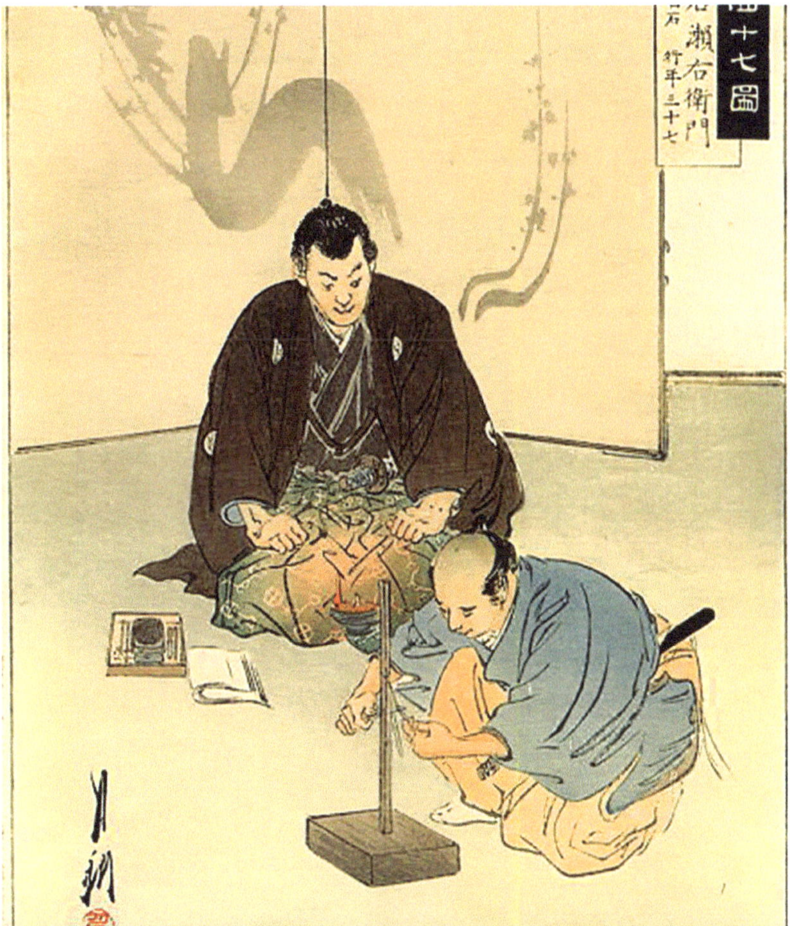

This samurai was one of the forty-seven ronin, who strictly followed the Bushido Code.

In times of peace, samurai worked hard to understand their lives and their place in the world. The **Zen Buddhism** philosophy helped them to do this. In fact, Zen Buddhism greatly affected the thoughts and culture of the samurai.

Zen Buddhism teaches spiritual growth through **meditation**. Meditation is a way of relaxing the mind and body with thought. Samurai who practiced Zen followed a strict physical and spiritual way of life. This practice led a samurai to **enlightenment**, or understanding of his own spirituality. Enlightenment allowed him to live without care or worry, even in times of great stress or pain.

Zen Gardens

For the more wealthy samurai, Zen was more than a personal philosophy—it was also used in the design of their homes and lands. A Zen garden was a different type of garden. Some did not even have plants—they were only rocks and sand.

The rocks and sand were representative of nature, either a river with islands, or the sky with mountains. These gardens were a source of great tranquility. People around the world still use Zen gardens both inside and outside their homes.

Zen gardens are often designed to be spaces for meditation. Some gardens even bring together the elements—water, earth, fire, sky, and air—so that nature is in balance.

Samurai were fierce warriors who faced death time and time again for their masters. They expected to be rewarded handsomely for their dangerous work.

The Bushido code states that all samurai must be loyal to their masters. Dedicated samurai fought hard in centuries-long struggles over control of Japan. However, they expected rich rewards for their efforts in battle. The most successful samurai were rewarded with the gift of land. Such rewards were an important part of the pact between the samurai and those they served. If a shogun or shugo neglected to give a samurai a proper gift for his loyalty, that warrior might break the Bushido code and turn on his superior.

Battles were fought for a number of different reasons. Some were waged against rebel samurai who fought against the power of the emperor or shogun. Others were fought between samurai clans who wanted to steal each other's land.

It is commonly believed that the sword was always the samurai's main weapon. In fact, the sword did not become the samurai's preferred weapon until the fourteenth century. Before that time, the bow and arrow was the samurai's weapon of choice. Early samurai fought mostly on horseback. They used their bows in battle to strike down their enemies from a distance.

Before fighting hand-to-hand battles, samurai were careful to choose the

BUSHIDO TIP

Samurai who had no masters were called *ronin*. They often wandered throughout Japan, challenging other samurai to battle. They viewed their skills as swordsmen as an important part of their spiritual growth.

This image of a samurai with a bow and arrow on horseback is probably close to what the first samurai looked like.

worthiest opponents. Choosing and defeating this opponent added glory to a samurai's victory. In fact, throughout samurai history, the most complete proof of success in battle was the presentation of the enemy's severed head to the master.

Attacking a Castle

One important aspect of samurai warfare was the **siege** of an enemy castle. A siege is the surrounding of a place by an

Sieges were common among samurai battles. This rooftop fight shows one way samurai warriors would invade an enemy's castle.

attacking army. The most powerful samurai built castles behind strong outer walls. These structures served as homes and fortresses to them, their families, and their men. When faced with an attack from a larger force, a samurai could retreat to the safety of his castle.

Starving an enemy was often the best weapon that an army had against a foe holed up in a fortress. It was a slow process to wait for an enemy to starve. Attacking samurai often tried to speed up the process by attempting direct attacks on a castle. Devices such as catapults and palisades were used during a siege. A catapult is a device that throws large stones. If aimed properly, a large enough stone could break apart a wall of a castle and allow a direct attack. A palisade is a large, movable tower. An army would build the tower the same height as the castle wall. The tower was then pushed to the edge of the wall. The samurai could then climb up through the palisade and get into the castle.

If all else failed, an attacking army could use tricks to draw its enemies out from a castle. For example, an attacking force would often offer a false peace treaty to an army inside a castle. If the army came out of the castle to discuss the treaty, they would be attacked on the open field.

The Age of Warring States

Throughout Japan's history, there have been many wars and battles. One violent period, known as the Age of Warring States, lasted from 1467 to 1590. During this time, there was no strong imperial government. Local rulers, known as **daimyo**, fought one another for control of small areas of land.

In addition to samurai, there were also a large number of foot soldiers that fought. These soldiers were peasants and farmers. A daimyo needed every man he could get for battle and was forced to train anyone who could fight.

Daimyo Akamatsu Masanori was an important general in the Onin War.

The armor used during this period was carefully crafted. It needed to be strong enough to resist the fire of a harquebus's shots and arrows. Each samurai wore a brightly colored banner on the back of his armor that was decorated with the badge of his master.

Daimyo Asano Naganori attacks Kira Yoshinaka in the Edo Castle.

The Loss of Bushido

Years of holding political power changed the samurai for the worse. By the late part of the seventeenth century, the codes of Bushido had been all but forgotten. In 1702, a shocking incident would remind Japan of the once-great ideals for which Bushido stood.

In 1700, Asano Naganori, the daimyo of Ako, lost his temper during an argument with Kira Yoshinaka. Kira was a powerful man in the court of the shogun. Asano drew his short sword and scratched the forehead of Kira. Asano was exiled and ordered to commit suicide. Forty-seven of Asano's samurai, now left without a master, swore to uphold their duties and **avenge** his death. For nearly two years, the samurai secretly plotted their attack on Kira's mansion. In December 1702, Oishi Yoshio, the chief of these ronin, led the raid on Kira's mansion. Oishi cut off Kira Yoshinaka's head and placed it on Asano's grave. This was to show that he fulfilled his duty to his master.

Only one of the ronin perished in the attack, but the other forty-six were ordered by the authorities to commit seppuku (ritual suicide) for their actions. While they were criminals, they also upheld the honor code of the samurai, which had been long lost. The tale of the "Forty-seven Ronin" has since become important in Japanese culture because it represents warriors restoring the lost honor of the samurai.

Influence from the outside world began to weaken the power of the samurai.

After centuries of fighting battles and wars that shaped the government and culture of Japan, the nineteenth century was very hard for the samurai. Outside forces began to threaten to end their rule.

For decades, Japan and the samurai had tried to resist the influence of European nations. These nations, such as Holland and Portugal, worked hard to establish trade with Japan. Japan did not want such contact with the Europeans. The Japanese were afraid that European culture would affect their way of life. However, most European nations had greater military strength than Japan.

Since Japan could not compete with the militaries of Western countries, the samurai government had a difficult decision to make. They needed to build the strength of their military to match that of the West. This meant that they had to accept some Western ideas and change their military systems. The samurai government found itself in an awkward position. The Japanese had to become more like the West in order to resist Western influence.

BUSHIDO TIP

According to some legends, Amakuni Yasutsuna is considered the father of the samurai sword. Yasutsuna created the curved blade after being inspired by a dream sent to him by the Shinto gods.

End of the Shogun Era

On January 3, 1868, the sixteen-year old Japanese emperor Mutsuhito of Japan held an early morning meeting. The emperor announced that shogun Tokugawa Keiki

This photograph of Mutsuhito was taken in 1873, just a few years after he ended the rule of the shoguns.

was to surrender his position of power. Shogun Keiki was the last of the shoguns.

For more than six hundred years, the shoguns had ruled Japan. There had always been an emperor, but during the time of the shoguns the emperor had served only as a religious and a cultural leader. The shoguns had always held the real power of government. The emperor's announcement marked the end of the shogun era.

As Japan industrialized, it became apparent that the samurai had no place in a modern society. They also had no

The Japanese forces adopted some Western techniques to create stronger defenses for their country.

place in Japan's new, modern army. By the 1870s, the samurai had become outdated. Some samurai turned to new professions. Others drifted aimlessly, wandering the countryside unable to do the job for which they were trained.

By 1905, Japanese culture had changed significantly, leaving no room for the ways of the samurai.

A common belief is that the way of the samurai is found in death. Samurai had always served their masters, even if it meant they had to die for them. In the end, the samurai class had to die for the good of their greatest master. That master was modern Japan.

The Samurai shaped the history of Japan for centuries, and they are still being remembered today. Countless paintings, stories, and films feature samurai warriors. For many, not just in Japan but also around the world, the noble ideals of a samurai warrior are still followed. Choosing to live with honor, understand duty, and practice **discipline** are all important lessons we can learn from the samurai.

The Seven Samurai, a film by the famous filmmaker Kurosawa, follows the fate of a group of samurai who protect a small town from destruction. It has become an international classic.

GLOSSARY

avenge To get revenge for.

Bushido A code of behavior followed by samurai.

clan A large group of related families.

daimyo Powerful samurai who ruled over small areas of land.

discipline Control over the way you or other people behave.

enlightenment To reach a state of understanding marked by the absence of desire or suffering.

harquebus An early type of rifle introduced to the samurai by European traders.

hostages People taken and held prisoner as a way of demanding money or other conditions.

martial arts Styles of fighting that come mostly from the Far East; for example, judo or karate.

medieval To do with the Middle Ages, the period between approximately AD 500 and 1050.

meditation Relaxing the mind and body through a regular program of mental exercise.

seppuku A ritual suicide by cutting open the stomach practiced by the Japanese samurai; hari-kari.

shogun The title given to the military leader of Japan from the twelfth to the nineteenth centuries.

shugo A powerful samurai who serves the shogun; a shugo also owns land.

siege The surrounding of a place, such as a city or a castle, to cut off its supplies and then wait for those inside to surrender.

Zen Buddhism A religion based on the teachings of Buddha; Buddhists strive to let go of material things to gain spiritual knowledge.

FIND OUT MORE

Books

Heppermann, Christine. *Samurai: Great Warriors*. Minneapolis, MN: ADBO & Daughters, 2013.

Hubbard, Ben. *The Samurai: Swords, Shoguns, and Seppuku*. Stroud, England: The History Press, 2014.

Lee, Adrienne. Samurai. *Legendary Warriors*. Mankato, MN: Blazers. 2013.

MacDonald, Fiona. *A Samurai! A Deadly Career You'd Rather Not Pursue*. You Wouldn't Want to Be. New York, NY: Scholastic Publishing, 2009.

MacDonald, Fiona. *Ancient Japan*. Hands-On History. San Francisco, CA: Armadillo Books, 2014.

Websites

The History Channel's Page on Samurai and Bushido
www.history.com/topics/samurai-and-bushido
In addition to the history of the samurai warriors, this page also has videos on samurai as well as a coroner's report on seppuku victims, a gallery of images, and additional links and information.

Japan-Guide.com's Official Sightseeing Guide to Samurai
www.japan-guide.com/e/e2127.html
Part of a larger website that highlights the history, geography, and attractions, this site contains a succinct history of the samurai of Japan.

The Samurai Archives Japanese History Page
www.samurai-archives.com
This page has links to historical articles about samurai, art depicting samurai, as well as a number of other resources.

INDEX

Page numbers in **boldface** are illustrations.